I Like the Seasons!

What Happens in Winter?

Sara L. Latta

Enslow Elementary
an imprint of

E | **Enslow Publishers, Inc.**

40 Industrial Road   PO Box 38
Box 398   Aldershot
Berkeley Heights, NJ 07922   Hants GU12 6BP
USA   UK
http://www.enslow.com

Words to Know

ice crystal (KRIH stuhl)— Water vapor that turns into ice.

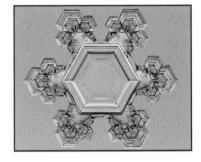

hibernation (hy bur NAY shun)—A time of deep sleep.

season (SEE zuhn)—One of the four parts of the year. Each season has a certain kind of weather.

tilt—To tip to one side. Earth tilts as it goes around the sun.

Earth is tilted.

Contents

What is winter?

Brrr—bundle up! It is winter, the coldest time of the year. Winter is one of the four seasons. The other seasons are spring, summer, and fall.

spring   summer   fall

4

winter

When is it winter in North America?

The earth goes around the sun one time each year. Earth **tilts** as it goes around the sun.

North Pole

Summer

Winter

Earth's path around sun

When the North Pole tilts away from the sun, it is winter in North America.

North Pole

Winter

When it is winter in the north part of Earth, it is summer in the south part of Earth!

Summer

Winter in North America lasts from around December 21 to March 21.

Why is winter weather cold?

The north part of Earth tilts away from the sun in winter. So, the sun's rays hit this part of Earth at an angle.

Rays on an angle are not as strong as rays that fall straight on Earth. So, winter sunlight is not as strong as summer sunlight.

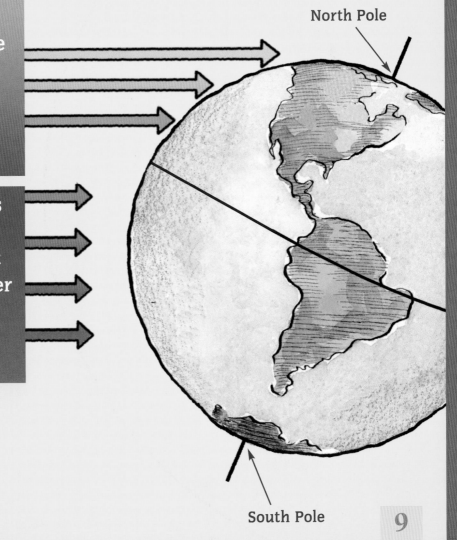

Here, the sun's rays hit Earth on an angle. These rays are not as strong. It is winter in the north part of Earth.

Here, the sun's rays hit Earth directly. Direct light is stronger than light at an angle. It is summer.

North Pole

South Pole

Why does winter weather bring snow and ice?

Earth gets fewer hours of sunlight in the winter. Less sunlight makes the air, water, and land get colder. When water is very cold, it freezes.

In the winter, water in the clouds can freeze into tiny ice crystals. The ice crystals form snowflakes. Water on lakes and ponds may also freeze in the winter.

These are photos of real snow crystals. They come in many shapes and sizes.

What happens to plants in the winter?

In the coldest parts of North America, trees and other plants may stop growing during the winter. They are resting. Their leaves may fall off. Plants live off the food they store in their roots.

Some trees stay green all year. They are called evergreens.

evergreen trees

Where do animals go in the winter?

There are not many growing plants for animals to eat in the winter. Some animals go to warmer parts of the earth where there is plenty of food.

Millions of monarch butterflies fly to Mexico for the winter.

Birds, squirrels, and other animals may search for seeds left on plants.

Bohemian
waxwing bird

What is hibernation?

Bears and other animals spend much of the cold winter months curled up in dens. They enter a deep sleep called hibernation.

This dormouse is hibernating.

They live off the fat they have stored in their bodies. When they come out of their dens in the spring, they are hungry!

A grizzly bear pulls leaves into its den.

What do people do in the winter?

Winter snow brings winter fun. If you live in a part of the country where it gets cold, you may go sledding or ice skating. You may build a snowman. Sometimes school is closed!

A salty solution to icy streets?

You will need:

- ❖ **2 ice cubes**
- ❖ **2 bowls or cups**
- ❖ **salt**
- ❖ **clock or watch**

1. Put one ice cube in each bowl.

2. Pour some salt over one ice cube. Add nothing to the second ice cube.

3. Check the ice cubes every ten minutes. Which ice cube melts the fastest? Can you guess why people put salt on the streets and sidewalks in the winter?

Learn More

Books

Berger, Melvin, Gilda Berger and Susan J. Harrison. *What Do Animals Do in Winter?* Ideals Publications, 1995.

Briggs, Martin, Jacqueline and Mary Azarian. *Snowflake Bentley.* Houghton Mifflin, 1998.

Glaser, Linda and Susan Swan. *It's Winter.* Millbrook Press, 2002.

Plourde, Lynn and Greg Couch. *Winter Waits.* Simon & Schuster Children's Publishing, 2000.

Williams, Judith. *Why Is It Snowing?* Berkeley Heights, N.J.: Enslow Publishers, Inc., 2005.

Web Sites

The National Center for Atmospheric Research and UCAR Office of Programs. Kids' Crossing.
<http://www.eo.ucar.edu/kids/index.html>

SnowCrystals.com
<http://www.its.caltech.edu/~atomic/snowcrystals/>

SnowSchool
<http://www.snowschool.org/kids/>

23

Index

Enslow Elementary, an imprint of Enslow Publishers, Inc.

Enslow Elementary® is a registered trademark of Enslow Publishers, Inc.

Copyright © 2006 by Enslow Publishers, Inc.

Library of Congress Cataloging-in-Publication Data

Latta, Sara L.
    What happens in winter? / Sara L. Latta.
      p. cm. — (I like the seasons!)
    Includes bibliographical references and index.
    ISBN 0-7660-2418-0 (hardcover)
    1. Winter—Juvenile literature. 2. Seasons—Juvenile literature. I. Title. II. Series
    QB637.8.L38 2006
    508.2—dc22

                                2005012446

Printed in the United States of America

10 9 8 7 6 5 4 3 2 1

To Our Readers: We have done our best to make sure all Internet Addresses in this book were active and appropriate when we went to press. However, the author and the publisher have no control over and assume no liability for the material available on those Internet sites or on other Web sites they may link to. Any comments or suggestions can be sent by e-mail to comments@enslow.com or to the address on the back cover.

Photo Credits: © 2005 Jupiter Images Corporation, pp. 4 (left, right), 13, 18, 20, 21, 22, 23; © 2005 Michael Conti/ AlaskaStock.com, p. 10; © age fotostock / SuperStock, pp. 2 (hibernation), 16; © Daryl Benson / Masterfile, pp. 2, 12; Mark Garlick/Science Photo Library, pp. 2 (bottom), 6–7; Richard Hutchings / Photo Researchers, Inc., p. 19; Paul Illes / Painet Inc., p. 4 (middle); Larry Landolfi / Photo Researchers, Inc., p. 8; Photos by Ken Libbrecht, pp. 2 (top), 11; © Stefano Nicolini / Animals Animals, p. 14; Steve Skjold / Painet Inc., p. 5; © Stouffer Productions / Animals Animals, p.17; James Zipp / Photo Researchers, Inc., p. 15.

Cover Photo: © 2005 Clark James Mishler/AlaskaStock.com

Science Consultant
Harold Brooks, Ph.D.
NOAA/National Severe Storms Laboratory
Norman, Oklahoma

Series Literacy Consultant
Allan A. De Fina, Ph.D.
Past President of the New Jersey Reading Association
Professor, Department of Literacy Education
New Jersey City University

24

Note to Parents and Teachers: The I Like the Seasons! series supports the National Science Education Standards for K–4 science. The Words to Know section introduces subject-specific vocabulary words, including pronunciation and definitions. Early readers may need help with these new words.